GOOGLE BARD FOR BUSINESS:

The Ultimate Guide to Unleashing AI-Powered
Productivity, Innovation, and Success

By

RENUTAASAN RAJAN

This comprehensive guide delves into the transformative potential of Google Bard for Business, equipping you with the knowledge and strategies to harness its power effectively.

CONTENTS

This book is an essential resource for business leaders, entrepreneurs, and anyone who wants to learn how to use Google Bard to improve their productivity, innovation, and success.

DISCLAIMER

This book is intended for educational purposes and to discuss using the Google Bard AI model. All trademarks and service marks mentioned in this book are the property of their respective owners.

The information and views presented in this book are those of the author and do not necessarily reflect the official opinion of Google AI or any other entity. The author has made every effort to ensure that the information in this book is accurate and up-to-date, but they assume no responsibility for errors or omissions.

No representation is made or implied that the reader will achieve the same results from using this book's suggested techniques, strategies, methods, systems, or ideas. The information in this book is presented for informational purposes only, and the reader is encouraged to use their judgment and to seek professional advice as needed.

The author assumes no responsibility or liability whatsoever for any direct or indirect losses incurred due to the use of the information contained in this book. By reading this book, the reader agrees that under no circumstances is the author responsible for any damages arising from the use or misuse of the information contained herein.

THANK YOU,

Dear Vasaki Mohan, Thusanth, and Thusantikaa,
Thank you for being my biggest supporters and
cheerleaders throughout book-writing. It was challenging,
especially when I spent long hours working on my
manuscript instead of spending time with you. But you
always believed in me and my dream, and I couldn't have
done it without you.

Family, business friends, and colleagues,
Thank you for your encouragement, love, and support. I'm
so grateful for your friendship and for always being there
for me, no matter what. I know I can always count on you.

Dear everyone else who has helped me along the way,
Thank you for all your support, big or small. I couldn't have
written this book without you. I especially want to thank the
people I didn't see who were still instrumental in helping
me complete this book. This includes my editors,

proofreaders, designers, and everyone else who worked behind the scenes to make this book a reality.

Google and Google Bard team,
Thank you for developing Google Bard, an excellent AI tool ideally suited for business people. It can assist them with various tasks, from generating documentation to brainstorming ideas.

I'm so grateful for everyone who helped me achieve my dream. This book is as much yours as it is mine.

INTRODUCTION

In the dynamic landscape of technological innovation, artificial intelligence (AI) chatbots have emerged as a transformative force, offering solutions, guidance, and companionship to users across the globe. Within the vast array of AI chatbots available, Google Bard stands out as a powerful tool specifically designed to address the needs of business professionals.

Having personally evaluated several AI chatbots, including ChatGPT, Microsoft CoPilot, and Google Bard, I have found Google Bard to be the most comprehensive and versatile tool for business users. Its ability to generate documentation, brainstorm ideas, and automate tasks makes it an invaluable asset for streamlining operations and enhancing productivity.

This book delves into the practical applications of Google Bard, empowering you to harness its potential to solve business problems, save time, generate creative ideas, and elevate customer service. Whether you're a seasoned entrepreneur or an aspiring business leader, you'll discover how Google Bard can revolutionise your approach to work and achieve remarkable results.

Before we embark on a journey to explore the myriad ways Google Bard can revolutionise your business, let's take a step back and examine the fascinating history of this groundbreaking AI chatbot. Understanding its origins and evolution will provide a deeper appreciation of its capabilities and pave the way for unlocking its full potential.

PART 1:

INTRODUCTION TO GOOGLE BARD

Welcome to the world of Google Bard—an innovative tool revolutionising how businesses approach tasks and challenges. In this exploration, we will embark on a journey through the chapters that unveil the essence of Google Bard. Chapter 1 delves into the fundamentals, addressing the pivotal question: What is Google Bard, and how does it work? As we venture further, Chapter 2 unfolds the myriad benefits businesses can reap by integrating Google Bard into their operations. Lastly, Chapter 3 presents compelling case studies showcasing companies that have not only embraced but thrived with the assistance of Google Bard. Join me as we unravel the transformative potential that Google Bard brings to the forefront of business dynamics.

Let's begin.

CHAPTER 1: WHAT IS GOOGLE BARD, AND HOW DOES IT WORK?

Google Bard is a new experimental chatbot that uses generative AI to help users with various tasks and challenges. Generative AI is a branch of artificial intelligence that can create unique and original content, such as text, images, music, etc., based on some input or prompt. Google Bard can understand natural language prompts and generate text-based responses that are relevant, informative, and creative. Google Bard can also access information from the web and use it to enrich its responses. This chapter will explore what Google Bard is and how it works for business.

Google Bard is powered by a deep neural network, a machine learning model that can learn from data and perform complex tasks. Google Bard uses a neural network called Transformer, a state-of-the-art natural language processing model. The transformer can encode the input prompt and decode the output response using attention, which allows the model to focus on the most relevant parts of the input and output. The Transformer can also generate long and coherent texts using self-attention, which enables the model to capture the context and structure of the text.

Google Bard is designed to aid users in addressing a range of tasks and challenges within the business domain. This includes idea generation, information retrieval, content creation, communication, and collaboration. Users can conveniently input their requests, and Bard will generate a tailored response based on the specific task and domain. To illustrate, here are examples of questions business owners can pose to Google Bard, accompanied by the response mechanism:

Question: "What are some innovative ideas for product development?"
Google Bard Reply: "Certainly! Here are a few innovative ideas for your product development..."

Question: "Retrieve information on market trends in the tech industry."
Google Bard Reply: "Sure, I found the latest market trends in the tech industry. Here is a summary of the key insights..."

Question: "Compose a draft for a business proposal."
Google Bard Reply: "Certainly! Here's a draft of your business proposal. Feel free to customise it according to your needs..."

Question: "Schedule a meeting with the marketing team next week."
Google Bard Reply: "Noted! I've scheduled a meeting with the marketing team for next week. Here are the details..."

Question: "Collaborate on a document with team members."

Google Bard Reply: "Absolutely! You can use the following link to collaborate with your team on the document..."

In addition to the aforementioned specific inquiries, business owners can harness the capabilities of Google Bard for assistance in the following areas:

- **Generating Creative Content:** Crafting marketing copy, blog posts, and social media content.

- **Language Translation:** Facilitating seamless communication across different languages.

- **Researching Topics:** Retrieving comprehensive information on various subjects.

- **Answering Customer Questions:** Providing timely and accurate responses to customer queries.

- **Troubleshooting Problems:** Offering support in identifying and resolving issues.

Google Bard proves to be a versatile and valuable tool for businesses. It empowers users to generate inspired, well-informed, and creative content. To experience the benefits of Bard, you can try it out by signing in with your Google Account using a supported browser.

CHAPTER 2: THE BENEFITS OF USING GOOGLE BARD FOR BUSINESS

Every AI chatbot brings unique advantages to its users, and when harnessed effectively with suitable prompts, these benefits can impact individual lives significantly. A notable addition to this landscape is Google Bard, an innovative experimental chatbot employing generative AI. Google Bard stands out by seamlessly comprehending natural language prompts and crafting responses that are not only pertinent but also possess a blend of informativeness and creativity.

What sets Google Bard apart is its ability to tap into the vast expanse of the internet, extracting valuable information to enhance the depth and relevance of its responses. In this chapter, we delve into the myriad benefits that Google Bard can offer businesses, showcasing how this advanced chatbot can be a game-changer in digital interactions.

Google Bard can help you save time and money.
Creating content for your business can take time, effort, and money. You may need to hire writers, editors,

researchers, designers, etc., to produce high-quality and engaging content for your business, such as articles, blogs, social media posts, newsletters, etc. However, with Google Bard, you can simply ask Bard to write something for you, and Bard will generate a suitable response for your audience, tone, and style. You can also edit and refine the generated content as you wish. This way, you can save time and money to invest in other aspects of your business.

Google Bard can help you improve your creativity and innovation. Generating new and creative ideas for your business can take time and effort. You may face writer's block, lack of inspiration, or competition. However, you can ask Bard for suggestions with Google Bard, and Bard will brainstorm some ideas for you. You can use these ideas as a starting point, a source of inspiration, or a way to explore different possibilities. For example, if you want to start a new online business, you can ask Bard for some online business ideas, and Bard will generate some possible options for you. You can choose the one that suits your skills, interests, and goals or combine different ideas to create something unique and innovative.

Google Bard can help you enhance your knowledge and skills. Retrieving relevant and reliable information from the web can take time and effort. You may need to search through multiple sources, filter out the noise, and verify the accuracy and credibility of the information. However, with Google Bard, you can simply ask Bard for some insights, facts, or data, and Bard will search the web and provide you with the information you need. You can also tell Bard to explain, summarise, or compare the information. For example, if you want to know more about the latest trends and opportunities in your industry, you can ask Bard for some insights, and Bard will provide you with some information from credible sources. You can then use this information to learn, grow, and improve your business.

In conclusion, Google Bard offers many benefits for businesses seeking to enhance their productivity, creativity, and knowledge base. Its ability to generate high-quality content, brainstorm innovative ideas, and provide comprehensive information makes it valuable for streamlining operations, fostering innovation, and expanding expertise. By embracing the power of generative AI through Google Bard, businesses can elevate their overall performance and achieve their desired goals.

In the upcoming chapter, let's delve into real-world case studies of brands leveraging Google Bard to enhance their business strategies and boost profitability. These practical examples will provide insights into how organisations have successfully incorporated Google Bard to achieve tangible business growth.

CHAPTER 3: CASE STUDIES OF BUSINESSES THAT HAVE SUCCESSFULLY USED GOOGLE BARD

Fortuitously, during the creation of this book, I uncovered compelling case studies from renowned brands that have harnessed the potential of Google Bard. This cutting-edge generative AI chatbot has emerged as a formidable tool for businesses aiming to elevate their operations, enhance productivity, and secure a competitive advantage. With its ability to generate fresh and original content, Google Bard empowers enterprises to streamline processes, optimise communication, and cultivate innovative ideas. Examining case studies involving Mozilla, Klippa, and Daffodil, we gain valuable insights into the transformative impact of Google Bard on the contemporary business landscape.

Mozilla: Fostering Open-Source Generative AI

Mozilla, a non-profit organisation dedicated to building privacy-focused software, has embraced Google Bard as a foundation for its open-source generative AI initiative. Mozilla aims to create a decentralised AI community that prioritises transparency, accountability, and trustworthiness, challenging the dominance of big tech companies in the AI domain. Google Bard is a starting point for Mozilla's endeavours, providing inspiration and guidance in pursuing a transparent, open-source, generative AI solution.

Klippa: Enhancing Content Creation and Customer Engagement

Klippa, a company specialising in document digitisation and processing, has harnessed Google Bard's capabilities to elevate its content creation and engagement strategies. Google Bard assists Klippa in crafting high-quality, engaging content for its website, blog, social media platforms, and newsletters. By delving into topics like document management, OCR, machine learning, and business automation, Google Bard helps Klippa establish itself as a thought leader in its industry. Additionally, Google Bard generates catchy headlines, slogans, and call-to-actions, enhancing Klippa's brand presence and customer engagement.

Daffodil: Fueling Creativity, Innovation, and Knowledge

Daffodil, a software engineering firm offering custom software development, cloud computing, AI, and IoT solutions, has employed Google Bard to fuel its creativity, innovation, and knowledge growth. Google Bard sparks new ideas for software products, features, designs, and strategies, propelling Daffodil's innovation pipeline. Furthermore, Google Bard efficiently retrieves relevant and reliable information from the web, presenting it naturally and conversationally and empowering Daffodil's team with the knowledge they need to excel. Google Bard also facilitates communication and collaboration within Daffodil and with its clients, partners, and colleagues, fostering a culture of knowledge sharing and innovation.

Google Bard has emerged as a transformative tool for businesses, enabling them to streamline operations, enhance productivity, and gain a competitive edge. Google Bard empowers companies to achieve their goals and excel in the ever-evolving marketplace through idea generation, information retrieval, content creation, and communication improvement. As generative AI technology advances, Google Bard is poised to play an increasingly significant role in shaping the future of business operations and innovation.

As we conclude this chapter, marking the end of Part 1, I trust you now have a comprehensive understanding of Google Bard and its benefits, backed by real-life case studies. Armed with this information, let's dive into the next section, which focuses on the practical applications of

Google Bard for specific businesses. We recognise that our readers hail from diverse industries, each seeking tailored and practical solutions to enhance their operations.

In Part 2, we will explore the intricacies of using Google Bard across various business classifications, addressing the unique needs and challenges different sectors face. Let's embark on this journey together.

PART 2:
USING GOOGLE BARD FOR SPECIFIC BUSINESS FUNCTIONS

With various businesses comes various needs.

Now that we've established a foundational understanding of what Google Bard is let's shift our focus to how Google Bard can specifically benefit your business. While I may still need to cover every business classification directly, I will provide a general overview that lets you understand how Google Bard can cater to your unique requirements.

Google Bard is a versatile tool that empowers users to enhance specific business functions, spanning sales and lead generation, customer service and support, product development and innovation, content creation and marketing, human resources, and employee management. Users can seamlessly instruct Bard to execute a task, and in response, Bard generates personalised and context-specific responses tailored to the customer, situation, and domain. Moreover, users enjoy the flexibility to edit and refine the induced reactions according to their preferences.

This part deepens the advantages and offers practical tips for incorporating Google Bard across various business functions. Furthermore, it showcases case studies of businesses successfully leveraging Google Bard for diverse purposes. By the end of this part, you'll have gained valuable insights into integrating Google Bard into your business operations, unlocking the potential of generative AI to foster inspiration, knowledge, and creativity.

CHAPTER 4: CONTENT CREATION AND MARKETING

This chapter holds a special place in my heart. Crafting content for marketing has evolved into a formidable challenge in today's fiercely competitive world. One must keep pace with and outthink competitors to stay ahead in this dynamic landscape.

In this era, content creation and marketing have emerged as indispensable tools for attracting, engaging, and converting potential customers. However, crafting compelling content is riddled with challenges—time constraints, creative roadblocks, and the constant demand for high-quality material. It's an intricate dance that businesses must master to thrive. Enter Google Bard, an innovative AI-powered chatbot that is a transformative solution. It streamlines the content creation process and elevates marketing strategies, offering a competitive edge to businesses navigating the complexities of the digital age.

Harnessing the Power of Generative AI for Content Excellence

Google Bard leverages the power of generative AI, a branch of artificial intelligence that can generate original and creative content based on specific inputs. This capability empowers businesses to overcome the traditional barriers of content creation and achieve remarkable results.

Benefits of Leveraging Google Bard for Content Creation and Marketing:

Enhanced Efficiency and Cost Savings: Google Bard streamlines the content creation, eliminating the need for extensive research, writing, and editing, saving businesses valuable time and resources. It can generate high-quality content in a fraction of the time it would take a human writer to 20produce, significantly reducing the overall cost of content creation.

Sparking Creativity and Innovation: Google Bard acts as a creativity catalyst, providing businesses with a steady stream of fresh and innovative content ideas. It can overcome writer's block and generate new perspectives, helping companies break creative barriers and develop unique content strategies.

Expanding Knowledge and Skill Advancement: Google Bard's ability to access and process vast information can significantly enhance businesses' knowledge bases. It can provide insights, facts, and data that would take hours or days to gather manually, empowering businesses to create more informative and authoritative content and establishing them as thought leaders in their respective industries.

Maximising Google Bard's Effectiveness through Effective Practices:

Crafting Effective Prompts: The quality of the prompt provided to Google Bard directly influences the outcome of the generated content. Clear, specific, and concise prompts that outline the content's topic, purpose, and desired format lead to better results.

Thorough Review and Editing: While Google Bard produces impressive results, businesses must carefully review and edit the generated content. This ensures that the content aligns with the brand's voice, style, and message while maintaining accuracy, professionalism, and adherence to industry standards.

Exploration and Experimentation: Google Bard's capabilities extend beyond traditional content formats, allowing businesses to explore new avenues like social media posts, email newsletters, and creative scripts. Experimentation with different prompts and styles can lead to unexpected and innovative content strategies that resonate with target audiences.

In the ever-evolving world of digital marketing, Google Bard empowers organisations to create engaging and impactful content that resonates with their target audiences and drives business success.

CHAPTER 5: CUSTOMER SERVICE AND SUPPORT

In this pivotal chapter, always remember: Your Customer is King.

The retention of customers hinges on the unwavering support they receive. In the vast business landscape, numerous adversaries lie in wait, ready to lure your clients away, even with products inferior to yours. Today, most customers prioritise superior customer service before or after purchasing products or services. Providing exceptional customer service has transcended being merely an aspect of success; it has become a crucial differentiator. Yet, delivering consistent, high-quality customer service can be challenging and resource-intensive. Enter Google Bard, an innovative AI-powered chatbot that emerges as a transformative solution for businesses seeking to streamline their customer service operations and enhance customer satisfaction.

Unleashing the Power of Generative AI for Customer -Centric Interactions

Google Bard harnesses the potential of generative AI, a subset of artificial intelligence capable of creating original and creative content based on specific inputs. This capability empowers businesses to overcome traditional barriers to customer service and achieve remarkable outcomes.

Benefits of Integrating Google Bard into Customer Service Strategies:

Enhanced Efficiency and Reduced Costs: Google Bard streamlines customer service processes, eradicating the need for extensive manual interventions and saving businesses valuable time and resources. It excels at generating comprehensive responses to customer inquiries and resolving issues promptly, significantly reducing the overall cost of customer service.

Elevated Customer Satisfaction and Loyalty: Google Bard's ability to comprehend and empathise with customers fosters positive interactions, increasing customer satisfaction and loyalty. It tailors responses to individual customer needs and preferences, making customers feel valued and understood.

Expanded Knowledge Base and Continuous Improvement: Google Bard's vast access to information empowers businesses to provide accurate and up-to-date responses to customer queries. It learns continuously from customer interactions, refining its responses and adapting to evolving customer needs.

Maximising Google Bard's Effectiveness through Strategic Implementation:

Crafting Effective Prompts: The quality of the prompt provided to Google Bard directly influences the outcome of the generated response. Clear, concise, and context-rich prompts that outline the customer query or issue lead to more effective interactions.

Thorough Review and Editing: While Google Bard produces impressive results, businesses must carefully review and edit the generated responses. This ensures that the answers align with the brand's voice, style, and message, maintaining accuracy, professionalism, and adherence to industry standards.

Continuous Experimentation and Optimization: Google Bard's capabilities extend beyond traditional customer service scenarios, allowing businesses to explore new avenues like proactive engagement, sentiment analysis, and feedback collection. Experimentation with different prompts and strategies can lead to unexpected and innovative customer service solutions.

Google Bard is a transformative tool for businesses seeking to elevate their customer service strategies and achieve customer-centric success. By leveraging its generative AI capabilities, companies can streamline customer interactions, enhance customer satisfaction, and continuously improve their service offerings. In the ever-evolving customer service landscape, Google Bard empowers organisations to deliver exceptional experiences that foster customer loyalty and drive business growth.

CHAPTER 6: SALES AND LEAD GENERATION

I strongly believe this could be your favourite chapter. Am I correct? This is where coffers fill, and leads come to life. In today's fiercely competitive business landscape, sales and lead generation are indispensable for growth, expansion, and success. However, navigating the complexities of these processes can be challenging, demanding, and time-consuming. Identifying and understanding customer needs, qualifying leads, nurturing relationships, and sealing deals require a deep understanding of customer behaviour, market trends, and effective sales strategies. This is where Google Bard emerges as a transformative tool, empowering businesses to streamline their sales and lead generation processes, enhance customer interactions, and drive business growth.

Leveraging Generative AI for Sales Excellence

Google Bard harnesses the power of generative AI, a branch of artificial intelligence that generates original and creative content based on specific inputs. This capability enables businesses to overcome traditional barriers to sales and lead generation, achieving remarkable results.

Key Benefits of Integrating Google Bard into Sales and Lead Generation Strategies:

Enhanced Efficiency and Cost Savings: Google Bard streamlines sales and lead generation processes, eliminating the need for extensive manual interventions. It quickly identifies and qualifies potential leads, generates personalised outreach messages, and nurtures relationships with prospects, significantly reducing the overall cost of sales and lead generation efforts.

Improved Customer Attraction and Conversion: Google Bard's ability to understand and empathise with customers fosters positive interactions, increasing customer attraction and conversion. It tailors sales pitches and proposals to individual customer needs and preferences, making customers feel valued and understood.

Expanded Market Insights and Customer Feedback: Google Bard's vast access to information empowers businesses to gain deeper insights into market trends, competitor strategies, and customer feedback. It can analyse data, identify patterns, and extract valuable insights that refine sales strategies, improve customer satisfaction, and drive business growth.

Maximising Google Bard's Effectiveness through Strategic Implementation:

Crafting Effective Prompts: The quality of the prompt provided to Google Bard directly influences the outcome of the generated response. Clear, concise, and context-rich prompts outlining the sales or lead generation task lead to more effective interactions.

Thorough Review and Refinement: While Google Bard produces impressive results, businesses must carefully review and refine the responses they generate. This ensures alignment with the brand's voice, style, and message while maintaining accuracy, professionalism, and adherence to industry standards.

Continuous Experimentation and Optimization: Google Bard's capabilities extend beyond traditional sales and lead generation scenarios, allowing businesses to explore new avenues like predictive analytics, sentiment analysis, and sales forecasting. Experimentation with different prompts and strategies can lead to unexpected and innovative sales and lead-generation solutions.

Google Bard is a transformative tool for businesses seeking to elevate their sales and lead generation strategies. By leveraging its generative AI capabilities, companies can streamline sales processes, enhance customer interactions, expand market intelligence, and drive business growth. In the ever-evolving sales and lead generation landscape, Google Bard empowers organisations to achieve remarkable results, propelling them to new heights of success.

CHAPTER 7: PRODUCT DEVELOPMENT AND INNOVATION

We crave new ideas, workflows, methodologies, services, or products to create customer value and achieve business goals. We call it Innovation. Companies consistently delivering groundbreaking products and services can stay ahead of the competition, captivate customers, and achieve remarkable growth. However, the path to innovation is often fraught with challenges, uncertainties, and complexities.

Identifying customer needs, generating creative solutions, and validating assumptions can be daunting. This is where Google Bard, an innovative AI-powered chatbot, emerges as a transformative tool, empowering businesses to streamline their product development processes, enhance customer insights, and unlock a new era of innovation.

Harnessing the Power of Generative AI for Innovation Breakthroughs

Google Bard leverages the power of generative AI, a branch of artificial intelligence that creates original and creative content based on specific inputs. This capability empowers businesses to overcome traditional product development and innovation barriers, achieving remarkable results.

Benefits of Leveraging Google Bard for Product Development and Innovation:

Enhanced Efficiency and Reduced Costs: Google Bard streamlines product development processes, eliminating the need for extensive manual interventions. It quickly identifies customer needs, generates creative solutions, and tests hypotheses, significantly reducing the overall time and cost of product development.

Improved Customer Value and Satisfaction: Google Bard's ability to understand and empathise with customers fosters positive interactions, increasing customer value and satisfaction. It tailors product concepts and designs to individual customer needs and preferences, making customers feel valued and understood.

Expanded Market Insights and Customer Feedback: Google Bard's vast access to information empowers businesses to gain deeper insights into market trends, competitor strategies, and customer feedback. It analyses data, identifies patterns, and extracts valuable insights that can be used to refine product concepts, improve customer experiences, and drive business growth.

Maximising Google Bard's Effectiveness through Strategic Implementation:

Crafting Effective Prompts: The quality of the prompt provided to Google Bard directly influences the outcome of the generated response. Clear, concise, and context-rich prompts outlining the product development or innovation task lead to more effective interactions.

Thorough Review and Refinement: While Google Bard produces impressive results, businesses must carefully review and refine the responses they generate. This ensures that the answers align with the brand's vision, values, and target audience while maintaining accuracy, professionalism, and adherence to industry standards.

Continuous Experimentation and Optimization: Google Bard's capabilities extend beyond traditional product development scenarios, allowing businesses to explore new avenues like idea generation, brainstorming sessions, and concept testing. Experimentation with different prompts and strategies can lead to unexpected and innovative solutions.

Google Bard is a game-changer for businesses seeking to elevate their product development and innovation strategies. By leveraging its generative AI capabilities, companies can streamline product development processes, enhance customer insights, and expand their knowledge base, propelling innovation efforts to new heights. In the ever-evolving world of product development, Google Bard empowers organisations to create groundbreaking products and services that capture market attention, foster customer loyalty, and drive business success.

CHAPTER 8: HUMAN RESOURCES AND EMPLOYEE MANAGEMENT

In today's fiercely competitive business landscape, attracting, retaining, and motivating a high-performing workforce is crucial for organisational success. Adequate human resources and employee management practices are essential for fostering a positive and productive work environment, driving employee engagement, and achieving business goals. However, managing the complexities of human resources and employee relations can be challenging, time-consuming, and demanding. This is where Google Bard emerges as a transformative tool, empowering businesses to streamline their HR processes, enhance employee insights, and revolutionise their approach to human capital management.

Harnessing the Power of Generative AI for HR Excellence

Google Bard leverages the power of generative AI, a branch of artificial intelligence capable of creating new and original content based on specific inputs. This capability enables businesses to overcome traditional human resources and employee management barriers, achieving remarkable results.

Key Benefits of Integrating Google Bard into HR and Employee Management Strategies:

Enhanced Efficiency and Cost Savings: Google Bard streamlines HR processes, eliminating the need for extensive manual interventions. It quickly identifies and qualifies candidates, generates personalised onboarding materials, and handles routine HR tasks, significantly reducing the overall cost of human resources management.

Improved Employee Attraction and Retention: Google Bard's ability to understand and empathise with employees fosters positive interactions, increasing employee attraction and retention. It tailors employee development plans, addresses performance concerns, and provides personalised recognition, making employees feel valued and understood.

Expanded Employee Insights and Feedback: Google Bard's vast access to information empowers businesses to gain deeper insights into employee needs, expectations, and motivations. It analyses employee surveys, identifies trends, and extracts valuable insights that can be used to refine HR strategies, improve employee satisfaction, and drive business growth.

Optimising Google Bard's Effectiveness through Strategic Implementation:

Crafting Effective Prompts: The quality of the prompt provided to Google Bard directly influences the outcome of the generated response. Clear, concise, and context-rich prompts outlining the HR or employee management task lead to more effective interactions.

Thorough Review and Refinement: While Google Bard produces impressive results, businesses must carefully review and refine the responses they generate. This ensures that the answers align with the company's culture, values, and policies while maintaining accuracy, professionalism, and adherence to industry standards.

Continuous Experimentation and Adaptation: Google Bard's capabilities extend beyond traditional HR scenarios, allowing businesses to explore new avenues like talent management, employee engagement, and diversity and inclusion initiatives. Experimentation with different prompts and strategies can lead to unexpected and innovative HR solutions.

Google Bard is a game-changer for businesses seeking to elevate their human resources and employee management strategies. By leveraging its generative AI capabilities, companies can streamline HR processes, enhance employee insights, and expand their knowledge base, propelling their human capital management efforts to new heights. In the ever-evolving world of HR, Google Bard empowers organisations to create a thriving and engaged workforce, driving business success and achieving long-term sustainability.

In this second part, you've clearly understood how Google Bard can be tailored to various business classifications, providing a broad overview. For a deeper dive, take a moment to sign in at bard.google.com and kick-start your search. Ensure your prompts are accurate, and witness Google Bard's ability to craft precise responses. Consider this your homework before we delve into the next part, where we explore the more advanced applications of Google Bard. While the topics might sound technical, I'll use casual terms to explain how everything works. Get ready for the next level of exploration!

PART 3:

ADVANCED APPLICATIONS OF GOOGLE BARD

Did you complete your homework? Just kidding!

If you've continued reading after finishing Part 2, I welcome you, and thank you for your continued motivation to explore this book. You're doing great! Part 3 comprises six chapters covering a range of fascinating topics: Building Chatbots and Virtual Assistants, Developing AI-powered Marketing Campaigns, Using Google Bard for Data Analysis and Decision-Making, Enhancing Education and Personalized Learning, Automating Content Creation and Translation, and Fostering Creativity and Artistic Expression. Don't worry; these are fascinating subjects, and I'm sure you'll enjoy reading about them all. The final part, "The Future of Google Bard," awaits you at the end with a thought-provoking prompt for your business.

Google Bard, a considerable language model (LLM) chatbot from Google AI, has emerged as a transformative force in artificial intelligence. Its ability to generate human-quallty text, translate languages, and answer questions informatively has paved the way for various applications across diverse industries.

Beyond its fundamental capabilities, Google Bard's potential extends far, enabling developers and users to harness its power for groundbreaking advancements. Here are some key areas where Google Bard is making a significant impact:

Building Chatbots and Virtual Assistants: Google Bard's conversational prowess makes it an ideal tool for crafting sophisticated chatbots and virtual assistants.

Developing AI-powered Marketing Campaigns: Google Bard's ability to generate creative text formats empowers marketers to tailor their messages more precisely.

Using Google Bard for Data Analysis and Decision-Making: Google Bard's capacity to process and analyse data makes it a valuable asset for extracting insights and informing strategic decisions.

Enhancing Education and Personalized Learning: Google Bard can provide personalised learning experiences, tailoring educational content to individual business people's needs.

Automating Content Creation and Translation: Google Bard's ability to generate human-quality text can streamline content creation and enable seamless translation.

Fostering Creativity and Artistic Expression: Google Bard's knack for generating creative text formats catalyses creativity, empowering individuals to explore new forms of expression.

Google Bard is a powerful force shaping the future of technology and society. Its ability to enhance human capabilities and drive progress across diverse domains positions it as a revolutionary tool with the potential to transform how we live and work.

Let's delve deeper into each key area to understand better how Google Bard can be an advanced tool for your business needs.

CHAPTER 9: BUILDING CHATBOTS AND VIRTUAL ASSISTANTS

Google Bard's ability to engage in natural, human-like conversations makes it an ideal tool for building sophisticated chatbots and virtual assistants. By leveraging Bard's conversational AI capabilities, developers can create interactive experiences seamlessly, bridging the gap between human and machine interactions.

Creating Engaging and Personalized Chatbots:

Bard's ability to understand context, adapt to different conversational styles, and generate personalised responses empowers developers to craft chatbots that effectively engage users. By utilising Bard's natural language processing (NLP) capabilities, developers can create chatbots that can:

- Understand user intent and provide context-aware responses
- Adapt their conversational style to suit individual users
- Personalize interactions based on user preferences and history

Enabling Seamless Customer Interactions:

Google Bard can seamlessly integrate into customer service applications, providing users with prompt, accurate, and personalised support. By empowering chatbots with Bard's capabilities, businesses can:

- Enhance customer satisfaction by delivering round-the-clock support

- Reduce customer support costs by automating routine inquiries

- Gather valuable customer feedback for continuous improvement

Expanding Virtual Assistant Functionality:

Google Bard can transform virtual assistants into more versatile and intelligent companions. By integrating Bard into virtual assistants, developers can:

- Enhance virtual assistants' ability to answer questions and provide information

- Enable virtual assistants to perform complex tasks and provide personalised recommendations

- Expand virtual assistants' ability to engage in natural and engaging conversations

Building Chatbots for Specific Industries:

Google Bard's versatility makes it suitable for building chatbots across various industries. Here are some examples:

- **Healthcare:** Google Bard can provide patients with information about their conditions, answer medical questions, and schedule appointments.

- **Education:** Google Bard can assist students with their studies, provide personalised tutoring, and answer questions about academic topics.

- **Finance:** Google Bard can help customers manage their finances, provide financial advice, and answer questions about financial products.

- **Retail:** Google Bard can provide customers with product recommendations, answer product-related questions, and assist with checkout.

As Google Bard continues to evolve, its potential for building chatbots and virtual assistants will only grow. By harnessing Bard's conversational AI capabilities, developers can create more sophisticated, personalised, and engaging chatbots that revolutionise how we interact with technology.

CHAPTER 10: DEVELOPING AI-POWERED MARKETING CAMPAIGNS

Artificial intelligence (AI) has ushered in a transformative era for marketing, revolutionising how businesses engage with their customers and achieve their marketing goals.

Google Bard, a large language model (LLM) chatbot developed by Google AI, stands at the forefront of this transformation, empowering marketers to create AI-powered marketing campaigns that are more effective, personalised, and data-driven than ever.

Unlocking the Power of Google Bard for AI-powered Marketing

Google Bard's capabilities extend far beyond its ability to generate text. Its ability to understand natural language, analyse vast amounts of data, and adapt to different audiences makes it an invaluable tool for developing AI-powered marketing campaigns. Here are some key ways Google Bard can create impactful marketing strategies:

1. **Generating Creative Marketing Content:** Google Bard excels at crafting compelling marketing content, including ad copy, social media posts, email campaigns, and product descriptions. Its ability to understand human language and generate creative text formats enables marketers to produce engaging, persuasive content tailored to specific audiences.

2. **Analysing Marketing Data and Gaining Insights:**
Google Bard's analytical capabilities make it a powerful tool for extracting valuable insights from marketing data. By analysing metrics such as click-through rates, conversion rates, and social media engagement, Bard can identify areas for improvement, optimise campaign strategies, and measure the effectiveness of marketing initiatives.

3. **Personalising the Customer Experience:** Google Bard's ability to analyse individual customer data and preferences enables marketers to create personalised marketing experiences that resonate with each customer. By tailoring messages, product recommendations, and content suggestions to specific customer profiles, Bard can enhance engagement, drive loyalty, and increase sales conversions.

4. **Automating Marketing Tasks and Processes:**
Google Bard can automate various marketing tasks, freeing marketers' time to focus on strategic planning and creative endeavours. By automating scheduling social media posts, generating personalised email campaigns, and optimising ad

campaigns, Bard can streamline marketing operations and improve overall efficiency.

5. **Predicting Customer Behavior and Preferences:** Google Bard's predictive capabilities allow marketers to anticipate future customer behaviour and preferences. By analysing customer data, purchase history, and online behaviour patterns, Bard can predict trends, identify potential customer segments, and proactively tailor marketing strategies to meet evolving customer needs.

6. **Enhancing Customer Support and Engagement:** Google Bard can power chatbots and virtual assistants to provide customers with real-time support, answer questions, resolve issues, and offer personalised recommendations. By providing 24/7 support and enhancing customer interactions, Bard can improve customer satisfaction and loyalty.

7. **Adapting to Changing Market Trends and Customer Preferences:** Google Bard's ability to learn and adapt makes it a valuable tool for navigating the dynamic marketing landscape. By continuously monitoring market trends, customer feedback, and competitor strategies, Bard can help

marketers adapt their campaigns and messaging to remain relevant and practical.

8. **Measuring the ROI of AI-powered Marketing Campaigns:** Google Bard can provide insights into AI-powered marketing campaigns' return on investment (ROI). By analysing campaign performance metrics and comparing results to traditional marketing strategies, Bard can help marketers quantify the impact of AI on their marketing efforts.

The Future of AI-Powered Marketing with Google Bard

As Google Bard continues to evolve and its capabilities expand, we can expect to see even more innovative applications of AI in marketing. Future advancements may include:

- **Emotionally intelligent marketing:** AI can analyse facial expressions, tone of voice, and other physiological data to gauge customer emotions, allowing marketers to create emotionally resonant campaigns.

- **Immersive marketing experiences:** AI can power augmented reality (AR) and virtual reality (VR) experiences, creating immersive marketing environments that engage customers on a deeper level.

- **Predictive customer intelligence:** AI can analyse vast customer data to predict future purchasing decisions, product preferences, and lifetime value.

- **AI-powered marketing automation platforms:** AI can automate entire marketing workflows, from strategy development to campaign execution and performance analysis.

Google Bard is poised to revolutionise the marketing industry, empowering businesses to create more effective, personalised, data-driven campaigns that drive customer engagement, increase sales, and foster long-lasting customer relationships. As AI continues to evolve, the possibilities for AI-powered marketing are limitless.

CHAPTER 11: USING GOOGLE BARD FOR DATA ANALYSIS AND DECISION-MAKING

Organisations constantly seek ways to extract meaningful insights from this vast information trove in a world awash with data. Google Bard, a groundbreaking large language model (LLM) chatbot developed by Google AI, offers a robust data analysis and decision-making solution, enabling businesses to make informed choices that drive growth and success.

Google Bard's Role in Data Analysis and Decision-Making

Google Bard's ability to process and analyse vast amounts of data, combined with its natural language processing (NLP) capabilities, makes it an invaluable tool for data-driven decision-making. Here are some key ways Google Bard can be utilised for data analysis and decision-making:

1. **Data Cleaning and Preparation:** Google Bard can assist in cleaning and preparing data for analysis, ensuring that the data is accurate, consistent, and error-free. By identifying and resolving data inconsistencies, Bard can improve the quality of data analysis and ensure that decision-making is based on reliable information.

2. **Exploratory Data Analysis (EDA):** Google Bard can perform exploratory data analysis (EDA) to comprehensively understand the data's

characteristics, patterns, and trends. By summarising data, identifying outliers, and visualising key relationships, Bard can help uncover hidden insights and inform further analysis.

3. **Statistical Analysis and Hypothesis Testing:** Google Bard can perform statistical analysis and hypothesis testing to draw statistically significant conclusions from the data. By applying statistical techniques and evaluating hypotheses, Bard can help validate or refute assumptions and inform strategic decision-making.

4. **Predictive Modeling and Forecasting:** Google Bard can build predictive models and forecast future trends based on historical data and current patterns. By analysing historical trends, identifying correlations, and applying machine learning algorithms, Bard can help businesses anticipate future outcomes and make proactive decisions.

5. **Data Visualization and Communication:** Google Bard can create compelling data visualisations to communicate insights and findings to stakeholders. Bard can transform complex data into easily understandable visualisations by generating charts,

graphs, and dashboards, facilitating informed decision-making.

6. **Real-time Data Monitoring and Alerts:** Google Bard can continuously monitor data streams and generate alerts for critical events or anomalies. By identifying deviations from expected patterns or thresholds, Bard can help businesses respond promptly to potential issues and make informed decisions in real time.

7. **Decision Support and Recommendation Systems:** Google Bard can provide decision support and recommendation systems to aid in complex decision-making processes. By analysing data, identifying factors, and evaluating potential outcomes, Bard can help businesses make informed choices that align with their strategic objectives.

Elevating Data-Driven Decision-Making with Google Bard

Google Bard is not just a tool for data analysis; it is a powerful catalyst for data-driven decision-making. By empowering businesses to extract meaningful insights from their data, Bard can help them:

- Identify new opportunities and market trends.
- Optimise resource allocation and improve operational efficiency
- Enhance customer satisfaction and loyalty.
- Gain a competitive edge in the marketplace.
- Make informed decisions that drive growth and success.

As Google Bard continues to evolve, its role in data analysis and decision-making will grow more prominent. Businesses embracing AI-powered data analysis will be well-positioned to navigate the dynamic business landscape, make informed choices, and achieve their strategic goals.

CHAPTER 12: ENHANCING EDUCATION AND PERSONALIZED LEARNING

Education is at a crossroads, facing the challenge of catering to diverse learning styles, adapting to individual needs, and providing engaging experiences that foster a deep understanding of concepts. Google Bard, a remarkable large language model (LLM) chatbot developed by Google AI, is essential to unlocking a new era of personalised learning and enhanced educational experiences.

Personalised Learning: Tailoring Education to Individual Needs

Google Bard's ability to analyse student data, assess learning gaps, and adapt to individual preferences empowers educators to create personalised learning experiences. By understanding each student's strengths, weaknesses, and learning styles, Bard can:

- **Craft customised learning plans:** Bard can generate personalised learning plans that align with individual student needs, providing a tailored roadmap for academic progress.

- **Provide real-time feedback:** Bard can offer immediate and personalised feedback on student work, helping them identify areas for improvement and reinforce understanding.

- **Adapt to individual learning styles:** Bard can adapt its teaching approach to suit different learning styles, providing visual, auditory, or kinesthetic explanations to cater to diverse preferences.

Enhancing Educational Experiences: Engaging and Interactive Learning

Google Bard's ability to generate creative text formats, translate languages, and answer questions informatively makes it an invaluable tool for enhancing educational experiences. By incorporating Bard into the classroom, educators can:

1. **Create interactive learning materials:** Bard can generate interactive quizzes, games, and simulations that bring concepts to life, making learning more engaging and memorable.

2. **Provide personalised explanations:** Bard can offer clear and concise explanations tailored to individual student needs, ensuring no one is left behind.

3. **Translate complex concepts:** Bard can seamlessly translate complex concepts into simpler terms, making them accessible to students with different language backgrounds.

4. **Promote cross-cultural understanding:** Bard can facilitate cross-cultural understanding by providing insights into diverse perspectives and cultures, enriching the learning experience.

Elevating the Role of Educators: Empowering Teachers

Google Bard's ability to automate repetitive tasks and provide real-time feedback frees up educators' time to focus on more personalised interactions with students. By streamlining administrative tasks and providing valuable insights, Bard can:

1. **Automate grading and assessment:** Bard can automate grading and assessment tasks, allowing educators to dedicate more time to providing personalised feedback and support.

2. **Identify at-risk students:** Bard can analyse student data to identify students at risk of falling behind, enabling early intervention and personalised support.

3. **Provide real-time feedback to educators:** Bard can provide real-time feedback on student

performance, helping them identify areas for improvement and adapt their teaching strategies.

Shaping the Future of Education with Google Bard

Google Bard represents a paradigm shift in education, paving the way for a personalised, adaptable, and engaging learning experience for all students. As Bard continues to evolve, we can expect even more innovative educational applications, including:

- **Predictive analytics:** Bard can analyse student data to predict future academic performance, enabling proactive interventions and personalised support.

- **Immersive learning experiences:** Bard can power augmented reality (AR) and virtual reality (VR) learning experiences, creating immersive environments that bring concepts to life.

- **Adaptive learning platforms:** Bard can power adaptive learning platforms that continuously adjust to individual student needs, providing a personallsed learning journey.

- **AI-powered tutors:** Bard can act as an AI-powered tutor, providing personalised instruction, answering questions, and offering real-time feedback.

Google Bard is poised to revolutionise education, transforming how we teach, learn, and interact with knowledge. By empowering educators with personalised learning tools and enhancing student engagement, Bard is paving the way for a future where education is more accessible, effective, and enjoyable for all.

CHAPTER 13: AUTOMATING CONTENT CREATION AND TRANSLATION

The demand for high-quality content is ever-increasing in today's fast-paced digital world. Businesses, organisations, and individuals must produce engaging, informative, and well-written content to stay ahead of the curve. However, creating and translating content can be a time-consuming and resource-intensive process. Here's where Google Bard, a powerful large language model (LLM) chatbot developed by Google AI, offers a transformative solution for automating content creation and translation.

Automating Content Creation: Generating Engaging Text Formats

Google Bard's ability to generate human-quality text in various formats makes it an invaluable tool for automating content creation. With its vast knowledge base and natural language processing (NLP) capabilities, Bard can

- **Write blog posts, articles, and social media content:** Bard can generate engaging and informative blog posts, articles, and social media content, saving time and effort for content creators.

- **Craft email campaigns:** Bard can create personalised and effective email campaigns that resonate with target audiences.

- **Develop product descriptions and marketing materials:** Bard can generate compelling product descriptions highlighting key features and benefits.

- **Compose creative text formats, such as poems, scripts, and musical pieces:** Bard can create a variety of innovative text formats, expanding the possibilities for content creation.

Enhancing Translation: Seamless Language Bridge

Google Bard's ability to translate languages accurately and fluently makes it an essential tool for automating content translation. With its multilingual capabilities, Bard can:

- **Translate websites and documents:** Bard can translate entire websites and documents into different languages, breaking down language barriers and expanding reach.

- **Localise content for global audiences:** Bard can localise content to suit specific regions and cultures, ensuring that messages resonate with local audiences.

- **Enable real-time multilingual communication:** Bard can power multilingual chatbots and virtual assistants, facilitating seamless communication across languages.

- **Translate technical and specialised content:** Bard can accurately translate technical and technological content, ensuring that information is accessible in multiple languages.

Streamlining Content Creation and Translation Workflows,

Google Bard's ability to automate content creation and translation tasks can significantly simplify workflows and enhance productivity. Bard can:

- **Reduce the time and effort required for content production:** Bard can automate repetitive tasks, such as writing first drafts and translating content, freeing content creators to focus on more strategic initiatives.

- **Improve content quality and consistency:** Bard can ensure that content is consistently high-quality and adheres to brand guidelines, maintaining a consistent brand voice.

- **Expand reach to global audiences:** Bard's translation capabilities enable businesses and organisations to reach a wider audience, expanding their global presence.

- **Reduce translation costs:** Bard can significantly reduce translation costs compared to traditional human services.

Shaping the Future of Content Creation and Translation

Google Bard is at the forefront of a revolution in content creation and translation, paving the way for a future where content is produced and translated more efficiently, accurately, and cost-effectively. As Bard continues to evolve, we can expect even more innovative applications in this domain, including

- **AI-powered content curation:** Bard can curate and summarise relevant information from various sources, saving time and effort for content creators.
- **Multilingual content optimisation:** Bard can analyse and optimise multilingual content for search engines, ensuring that content is visible and relevant to global audiences.

- **AI-powered translation tools for specific industries:** Bard can be adapted to particular sectors, such as law, medicine, and finance, providing specialised translation services.

- **Real-time translation for multilingual meetings and conferences:** Bard can enable real-time translation during multilingual meetings and conferences, breaking down language barriers and facilitating global collaboration.

With its remarkable content creation and translation capabilities, Google Bard is poised to revolutionise how we produce, consume, and share information across languages and cultures. By automating repetitive tasks, enhancing content quality, and expanding global reach, Bard empowers businesses, organisations, and individuals to create and translate content more effectively than ever.

CHAPTER 14: FOSTERING CREATIVITY AND ARTISTIC EXPRESSION

Creativity and artistic expression are fundamental aspects of human experience, enabling us to explore the world, communicate emotions, and create new forms of beauty and meaning. Google Bard, a groundbreaking large language model (LLM) chatbot developed by Google AI, offers a powerful tool for fostering creativity and artistic expression, empowering individuals to explore their artistic potential and redefine the boundaries of creative exploration.

Sparking Creativity: Igniting the Artistic Spark

Google Bard's ability to generate creative text formats, translate languages, and answer questions informatively makes it an invaluable tool for sparking creativity. By providing a platform for experimentation, exploration, and expression, Bard can help individuals

- **Overcome creative blocks:** Bard can help individuals overcome creative blocks by providing fresh perspectives, suggesting new ideas, and offering prompts to stimulate creativity.
- **Explore new creative genres:** Bard can help individuals explore new creative genres, such as poetry, songwriting, and scriptwriting, expanding their artistic horizons.

- **Receive constructive feedback:** Bard can provide constructive feedback on creative work, helping individuals refine their skills and artistic voice.

Enhancing Artistic Expression: Expanding Artistic Possibilities

Google Bard's ability to understand and manipulate language makes it a powerful tool for enhancing artistic expression. By providing a versatile platform for creative exploration, Bard can help individuals:

- **Craft compelling narratives:** Bard can assist in crafting compelling narratives, whether for novels, screenplays, or short stories, bringing characters and stories to life.
- **Generate creative text formats:** Bard can generate a variety of innovative text formats, including poems, scripts, musical pieces, emails, letters, and more, expanding the possibilities for artistic expression.
- **Translate creative works:** Bard can translate creative works into different languages, enabling artists to share their work with a broader audience and expand their global reach.
- **Collaborate on creative projects:** Bard can facilitate collaboration on creative projects, bringing together artists from diverse backgrounds to create unique and innovative works.

Nurturing Artistic Communities: Fostering Connections and Inspiration,

Google Bard can foster connections and inspire creativity among artists by providing a platform for sharing ideas, exchanging feedback, and collaborating on projects. Bard can:

- **Connect artists with like-minded individuals:** Bard can connect artists with like-minded individuals, creating a network of support and inspiration.
- **Facilitate online workshops and discussions:** Bard can facilitate online workshops and discussions, providing opportunities for artists to learn from each other and share their knowledge.
- **Organise virtual art exhibitions:** Bard can organise exhibitions showcasing artists' work worldwide.
- **Promote artistic diversity:** Bard can promote creative diversity by highlighting artists' work from underrepresented backgrounds and marginalised communities.

Revolutionising the Creative Landscape with Google Bard

Google Bard is poised to revolutionise the creative landscape, empowering individuals to explore their artistic potential and redefine the boundaries of creative expression. As Bard continues to evolve, we can expect even more innovative applications in creativity, including

- **AI-powered art generation:** Bard can generate unique and original artworks, such as paintings, sculptures, and digital art.

- **AI-powered music composition:** Bard can compose original music pieces in various genres, showcasing its versatility and creativity.

- **AI-powered storytelling tools:** Bard can assist in developing and refining story plots, characters, and narratives, enhancing the storytelling process.

- **AI-powered creative assistants:** Bard can act as an AI-powered creative assistant, providing suggestions, prompts, and feedback throughout the creative process.

With its extraordinary ability to foster creativity and artistic expression, Google Bard empowers individuals to unleash their artistic potential, explore new creative avenues, and contribute to a world enriched by the diversity of expression. Bard is paving the way for a future where creativity knows no bounds by providing a platform for experimentation, exploration, and collaboration.

Finally, you've made it! You've completed Part 3, and I'm confident you've gained valuable insights into the advanced applications of Google Bard. While this book covers a lot, remember that Google Bard is continually evolving, and there may be even more advanced applications and benefits to discover. Always stay updated and take your time to visit my website by searching my name, Renutaasan, on Google or Google Bard. You'll land at www.renutaasan.com, where I frequently share many technology-related articles, including tips and tricks.

Now, onto the final chapter, I've gathered a wealth of information on the Future of Google Bard in Business. Top technologies and mentors release many articles. Together, let's explore the future of Google Bard in this book's next and final part.

PART 4:

THE FUTURE OF GOOGLE BARD AND AI IN BUSINESS

\

The future is unpredictable, yet we find insight in articles released by top technology minds. Visionaries such as Elon Musk, CEO of Tesla and SpaceX; Andrew Ng, Co-founder of Coursera and a leading AI researcher; Fei-Fei Li, a professor at Stanford and the co-director of the Stanford Artificial Intelligence Lab; Yoshua Bengio, a computer scientist and professor at the University of Montreal; Demis Hassabis, Co-founder of DeepMind; Satya Nadella, CEO of Microsoft; Kai-Fu Lee, a venture capitalist; Jeff Dean, a Google Senior Fellow in the Research Group; Gary Marcus, a cognitive scientist, author, and entrepreneur; and Max Tegmark, a physicist and author, have shared their perspectives on the future of AI. They acknowledge both the potential benefits and challenges it brings to businesses. Countless teams are working tirelessly to find the best solutions, and we anticipate witnessing significant progress soon.

Enhanced Customer Experiences:

Google Bard's ability to understand and respond to natural language is invaluable for improving customer interactions. By providing personalised product recommendations, resolving customer inquiries efficiently, and offering proactive support, Bard can elevate the customer experience to new levels of satisfaction and loyalty.

Streamlined Operations and Decision-Making:

Bard's data analysis and decision-making capabilities can significantly improve operational efficiency across various business functions. By analysing vast amounts of data, Bard can identify patterns, predict trends, and provide actionable insights to inform strategic decision-making. This can lead to optimised resource allocation, reduced costs, and improved organisational performance.

Increased Creativity and Innovation:

Bard's creative prowess can spark new ideas and foster innovation within businesses. By generating fresh perspectives, assisting with creative tasks, and exploring unique concepts, Bard can empower businesses to develop groundbreaking products, services, and strategies that set them apart.

Personalised Learning and Development:

Bard's ability to tailor learning experiences to individual needs can transform employee training and development. By providing customised learning paths, adaptive feedback, and personalised recommendations, Bard can enhance employee skills, knowledge, and performance, contributing to a more skilled and adaptable workforce.

Ethical Implications of AI in Business:

The rapid adoption of AI in business raises critical ethical considerations. Companies must ensure that AI systems are developed and used responsibly, with transparency, fairness, and accountability being paramount. Ethical considerations include:

- Avoiding bias and discrimination: AI systems must be designed to prevent and mitigate bias, ensuring they treat all individuals fairly and equitably.
- Protecting privacy and security: AI systems must handle sensitive personal data carefully, adhering to strict privacy and security protocols.
- Ensuring transparency and explainability: AI systems should be designed to be transparent and explainable, allowing users to understand the reasoning behind decisions made by AI algorithms.

Preparing for the Future of Work in an AI-Powered Economy:

- The AI-powered economy will demand new skills and competencies from the workforce. Businesses must proactively prepare for this shift by:
- Reskilling and upskilling employees: Providing employees with opportunities to learn and develop new skills relevant to the AI-powered workplace.
- Fostering a culture of lifelong learning: Encouraging employees to embrace continuous learning and adapt to the ever-evolving technological landscape.
- Human-AI collaboration: Emphasizing the importance of human-AI partnership, recognising that AI complements and enhances human capabilities.

Google Bard and AI represent a transformative force in the business world. By responsibly and ethically leveraging AI's potential, businesses can reap significant benefits in enhanced customer experiences, streamlined operations, increased creativity, and a more skilled workforce. As AI continues to evolve, companies that embrace AI-powered solutions will be well-positioned to thrive in the dynamic and competitive future of work.

CHAPTER 15: THE ETHICAL IMPLICATIONS OF USING AI IN BUSINESS

The ethical implications of using AI in business are important and complex. AI can bring many benefits to businesses, such as improving efficiency, productivity, innovation, and customer satisfaction. However, AI can pose many challenges and risks, such as bias, privacy, accountability, transparency, and social impact. Therefore, businesses must consider AI's technical, legal, ethical, and moral aspects.

Some fundamental ethical principles companies should follow when using AI are respecting **human dignity and autonomy.** AI should respect the inherent worth and dignity of every human being and protect their rights and freedoms. AI should not harm, manipulate, or exploit humans or infringe on their privacy and consent.

Promote human welfare and well-being. AI should contribute to the common good and the public interest and enhance human quality of life and well-being. AI should not cause harm, discrimination, or injustice to humans or endanger their health and safety.

Ensure fairness and justice. AI should be fair and impartial and avoid or mitigate any bias, prejudice, or discrimination. AI should be transparent and explainable and allow for human oversight and accountability. AI should also be inclusive and accessible and respect diversity and pluralism—fostering **trust and reliability.** AI should be reliable and trustworthy and perform as intended and expected. AI should be secure and resilient and protect against malicious attacks or misuse. AI should also be honest and truthful and avoid deception or fraud.

These ethical principles can help businesses use AI responsibly and sustainably and build stakeholder trust and confidence. However, applying these principles in practice can be challenging, as different situations may require different trade-offs or balances. Therefore, businesses must adopt a human-centric and stakeholder-oriented approach to AI ethics and engage in continuous dialogue and collaboration with all relevant parties, such as customers, employees, regulators, and society. By doing so, businesses can ensure that they are using AI not only for their benefit but also for the benefit of humanity.

CHAPTER 16: PREPARING FOR THE FUTURE OF WORK IN AN AI-POWERED ECONOMY

Preparing for the future of work in an AI-powered economy is a timely and relevant topic, as artificial intelligence (AI) is transforming many industries and sectors. AI can bring many benefits, such as increasing efficiency, productivity, innovation, and customer satisfaction. However, AI can pose many challenges and risks, such as displacing workers, creating ethical dilemmas, and requiring new skills and competencies.

To prepare for the future of work in an AI-powered economy, it is essential to understand AI's current and potential impacts on the labour market, the education system, and society at large. It is also necessary to adopt proactive and collaborative strategies to leverage the opportunities and mitigate the threats of AI. Some of the critical steps that can be taken are:

They are developing a lifelong learning mindset and culture. AI is constantly evolving and creating new demands and possibilities for work. Therefore, workers must be adaptable and resilient and continuously update their knowledge and skills. This can be done by engaging in formal and informal learning opportunities, such as online courses, certifications, mentoring, and peer learning.

They are fostering human-centric and interdisciplinary skills. AI is not a substitute for human intelligence, creativity, and empathy. Instead, it is a complement and an enabler. Therefore, workers must develop and enhance their soft skills, such as communication, collaboration, problem-solving, and critical thinking. They must also acquire and integrate knowledge and skills from different domains, such as science, technology, engineering, arts, and mathematics (STEAM).

They are embracing diversity and inclusion. AI can be a powerful tool for advancing social and economic justice and a source of bias and discrimination. Therefore, workers must respect stakeholders' diverse perspectives and needs, such as customers, colleagues, and communities. They must also ensure that AI is designed and used fairly, transparently, and accountable, reflecting and respecting society's values and norms.

They are collaborating across sectors and boundaries. AI is a complex and dynamic phenomenon that requires collective and coordinated action from various actors, such as governments, businesses, educators, researchers, and civil society. Therefore, workers need to build and maintain strong and trustful relationships with different partners and share their expertise, resources, and best practices. They also need to participate in and contribute to the public dialogue and policy-making on AI and advocate for the common good and the public interest.

These are some ways that workers can prepare for the future of work in an AI-powered economy.

Done. It's complete. I've shared many important insights about Google Bard, breaking it into four parts and 16 chapters. Some chapters are straightforward, while others may require practical testing to grasp the concepts thoroughly. Most importantly, as I initially emphasised, Google Bard is a fantastic tool for business growth and saving time and money.

Ensure you use the correct prompts, and perhaps, if fate allows, your business might be featured in my next book under a case study showcasing how it leveraged Google Bard to achieve its targets.

As I write this final paragraph, I've learned that Google has launched its new tool, Duet Ai, which is similar to Google Bard but more advanced in productivity. Always stay updated with the latest tech tools; try new ones that can benefit your business, some of which may be free. For chargeable people, stick to a yearly budget and subscribe if it aligns with your business needs.

Among other tech mentors, I will continue my search for the future of Google Bard and other AI chatbots. Drop by my website, www.renutaasan.com, for the latest updates, or simply ask Google Bard, "Can you list the latest tools I can use for my business to lead the marketing team?" It will display ten or more suggestions.

Once again, thank you for taking the time to read my first book, and I appreciate your blessings for upcoming books. Let me end with my hashtag, #growwithrr.

BONUS:

BUSINESS PROMPTS

Prompts play an essential role in any AI chatbot to get accurate reports. Wrong or incomplete prompts can lead to inaccurate information. Ask the right questions and use prompts according to your business needs. As a bonus for readers, I will highlight a few essential business prompts based on business classification. Below sample prompts will give you a kickstart idea to begin your search journey with Google Bard.

General Business Management:

1. "Generate a comprehensive business plan for a startup in the tech industry."
2. "Help me draft a compelling mission statement for my business."
3. "Create a list of key performance indicators (KPIs) for tracking business success."
4. "Assist in developing a strategic marketing plan for the next quarter."
5. "Generate ideas for improving employee engagement and morale."

Marketing and Sales:

6. "Suggest creative content ideas for our next social media campaign."
7. "Help me optimise my Google Ads strategy for better ROI."
8. "Generate a list of potential influencers for a product collaboration."
9. "Create a sales script for our latest product or service."
10. "Generate email copy for a targeted marketing campaign."

Finance and Accounting:

11. "Assist in creating a budget for the upcoming fiscal year."
12. "Generate financial projections for the next five years."
13. "Provide insights on cost-cutting strategies without compromising quality."
14. "Help me analyse and interpret my financial statements."
15. "Generate a cash flow forecast for the next quarter."

Human Resources:

16. "Assist in developing an employee training program."

17. "Create a job description template for a new position in our company."

18. "Generate interview questions for hiring a senior manager."

19. "Suggest employee retention strategies for a small business."

20. "Help me draft a fair and comprehensive employee handbook."

Operations and Logistics:

21. "Optimize our supply chain for better efficiency."

22. "Generate ideas for improving warehouse organisation and logistics."

23. "Assist in creating a contingency plan for unexpected disruptions in operations."

24. "Help me implement lean principles in our manufacturing process."

25. "Generate ideas for improving customer service processes."

Technology and IT:

26. "Suggest cybersecurity measures to enhance our data protection."

27. "Create a plan for migrating our business to the cloud."

28. "Generate ideas for implementing AI in our customer support processes."

29. "Help me choose the right project management software for our team."

30. "Assist in developing an IT strategy aligned with our business goals."

E-commerce:

31. "Optimize product listings for better visibility on online marketplaces."

32. "Generate ideas for a customer loyalty program for our e-commerce store."

33. "Help me create a compelling product description for a new product launch."

34. "Assist in setting up an effective abandoned cart email campaign."

35. "Generate ideas for increasing conversion rates on our website."

Health and Wellness:

36. "Create a wellness program for employees to enhance workplace well-being."

37. "Generate content ideas for promoting health products on social media."

38. "Help me develop a fitness challenge for our company."

39. "Assist in creating a nutrition guide for our employees."

40. "Suggest mental health resources for our workplace."

Hospitality and Tourism:

41. "Create a marketing plan to attract more tourists to our destination."

42. "Generate ideas for improving customer experience in our hotel."

43. "Help me develop a loyalty program for our restaurant."

44. "Assist in optimising our booking system for better efficiency."

45. "Suggest strategies for managing online reviews and reputation."

Real Estate:

46. "Generate ideas for a real estate marketing campaign targeting first-time homebuyers."

47. "Help me create a virtual tour for our property listings."

48. "Assist in developing a property management plan for rental units."

49. "Create a social media strategy for a real estate agency."

50. "Generate ideas for staging homes to increase market value."

Education and Training:

51. "Develop an online course curriculum for our training program."
52. "Assist in creating engaging educational content for our audience."
53. "Generate ideas for gamifying our training modules."
54. "Help me optimise our e-learning platform for user engagement."
55. "Create a plan for measuring the effectiveness of our training programs."

Legal and Compliance:

56. "Generate a checklist for ensuring GDPR compliance in our business."
57. "Assist in creating a code of conduct for our employees."
58. "Help me draft a partnership agreement for a new business venture."
59. "Create a risk management plan for our company."
60. "Suggest strategies for ensuring workplace diversity and inclusion."

Sustainability and Environmental Initiatives:

61. "Generate ideas for implementing eco-friendly practices in our business."
62. "Help me develop a sustainability report for our stakeholders."
63. "Assist in creating a plan to reduce our carbon footprint."
64. "Suggest suppliers and vendors with sustainable practices."
65. "Create a communication strategy for promoting our green initiatives."

Manufacturing and Production:

66. "Optimize our production schedule for better efficiency."
67. "Generate ideas for implementing automation in our manufacturing process."
68. "Help me create a quality control plan for our products."
69. "Assist In developing a product lifecycle management strategy."

70. "Suggest strategies for reducing waste in our production process."

Fashion and Apparel:

71. "Create a social media content calendar for our fashion brand."
72. "Generate ideas for a sustainable fashion initiative."
73. "Help me optimise our online store for a better shopping experience."
74. "Assist in creating a fashion show marketing plan."
75. "Suggest strategies for collaborating with influencers in the fashion industry."

Nonprofit and Social Impact:

76. "Generate ideas for a fundraising campaign to support our cause."
77. "Help me create a social media strategy to raise awareness about our nonprofit."
78. "Assist in developing a community outreach program."
79. "Create a plan for measuring the impact of our social initiatives."
80. "Suggest partnerships with other nonprofits for collaborative projects."

Food and Beverage:

81. "Generate ideas for a menu revamp to attract more customers."
82. "Help me develop a food safety and hygiene protocol."
83. "Assist in creating a marketing plan for a new restaurant opening."
84. "Suggest strategies for managing inventory in a restaurant."
85. "Create a plan for sourcing local and sustainable ingredients."

Beauty and Wellness:

86. "Optimize our salon's online presence through social media."
87. "Generate ideas for a spa promotion to attract new clients."
88. "Help me create a loyalty program for our beauty products."
89. "Assist in developing a wellness retreat package."
90. "Suggest strategies for implementing eco-friendly practices in our salon."

Construction and Home Improvement:

91. "Generate ideas for a marketing campaign targeting homeowners."

92. "Help me create a project management plan for a construction project."

93. "Assist in developing a safety protocol for construction sites."

94. "Create a plan for incorporating sustainable materials in our projects."

95. "Suggest strategies for improving client communication during construction."

Technology Startups:

96. "Optimize our software development process for faster releases."

97. "Generate ideas for a tech product launch campaign."

98. "Help me create a pitch deck for potential investors."

99. "Assist in developing a user acquisition strategy for our app."

100. "Suggest strategies for building a strong tech team."

Feel free to mix and match these prompts based on your business needs and goals!

UNDERSTANDING LLM & NLP

Both NLP and LLM are involved in the fascinating world of computers understanding and processing human language, but they approach it from different angles.

NLP is a broader field that encompasses a vast range of techniques and tasks related to understanding and manipulating human language. It focuses on equipping machines with the ability to grasp the meaning and intention behind language, similar to how humans do. NLP has diverse applications across various industries, from chatbots and machine translation to spam filtering and automated content moderation.

LLM, on the other hand, is a specific type of AI model trained on massive amounts of text data. It focuses on generating impressive and creative text formats, such as answering open-ended questions, translating languages, or writing different kinds of creative content. LLMs are still evolving, but they show promise in areas like personalized education, generating realistic chatbots, and assisting people with disabilities in communication. Ultimately, NLP and LLM complement each other, as NLP provides the foundation for understanding language, while LLMs leverage that understanding to create human-quality text.

MY INSPIRATION

Since I was 13, I have immersed myself in the world of books, spending countless hours in the school library. This habit not only supported my studies but fueled my passion for self-improvement. At 16, my dedication caught the attention of my teacher, who appointed me as a library committee member. After seven months, I assumed the role of secretary until the culmination of my primary school journey. Subsequently, the Malaysia National Library became my haven, housing millions of books.

My aspiration was simple yet profound: to see on a library shelf a source of benefit for someone unknown. However, at that time, I needed to learn what to write or the topics to explore.

With a 20-year background in the technology business since the dawn of websites like Facebook, Hi5, LinkedIn, and more, I've trained over 15,000 small and medium business owners. Witnessing their success stories has been immensely rewarding. Drawing on two decades of business experience and with more chapters yet to unfold, I bring you this book confident that it captures the current trend and is backed by my substantial knowledge.

In the words of Dr A.P.J. Abdul Kalam, the Indian aerospace scientist and 11th President of India, "Dream, dream, dream. Dreams transform into thoughts, and thoughts result in action." With this philosophy guiding my journey, I eagerly anticipate what lies ahead.

REFERENCE

Part 1: Source

Introduction to Google Bard

(1) Google Bard logo :

https://logowik.com/content/uploads/images/google-bard38

72.logowik.com.webp

Chapter 3: Source

(1) Mozilla Open Source AI To Challenge ChatGPT & Bard
- Search Engine Journal.

https://www.searchenginejournal.com/mozilla-open-source-
ai/482981/.

(2) What is Google Bard, and how can you use it? - Klippa.

https://www.klippa.com/en/blog/information/what-is-google-
bard/.

(3) All About Google Bard: The New Disruptor in
Conversational AI - Daffodil.

https://insights.daffodilsw.com/blog/all-about-google-bard.

(4) KPMG lodges complaint after AI-generated material
was used to implicate ....

https://www.theguardian.com/business/2023/nov/03/kpmg-
ai-complaint-non-existent-scandal-ai-case-studies-google-
bard.

Chapter 15: Source

(1)
https://bing.com/search?q=The+ethical+implications+of+
using+AI+in+business.

(2) Ethical implications of AI and the future of work |
Deloitte Insights.
https://www2.deloitte.com/us/en/insights/focus/human-capi
tal-trends/2020/ethical-implications-of-ai.html.

(3) What Does Ethical AI Mean for Your Business? - Levity.
https://levity.ai/blog/ethical-ai-for-business.

(4) AI Ethical Issues in Business | Maryville Online.
https://online.maryville.edu/blog/ai-ethical-issues/.

(5) AI Ethics Are a Concern. Learn How You Can Stay
Ethical - G2. https://learn.g2.com/ai-ethics.

(6) The ethical considerations of using AI in business. -
Medium.
https://medium.com/@OfentseManchidi/the-ethical-conside
rations-of-using-ai-in-business-fa65879c901f.

(7) undefined. https://www.iso.org/news/ref2454.html.

(8) undefined.
https://www.worldgovernmentsummit.org/docs/default-sour
ce/default-document-library/deloitte-wgs-report-en-lq.pdf?s
fvrsn=1acfc90b_0.

(9) undefined.
https://www.thinkautomation.com/automation-ethics/are-ai-
ethics-impossible/.

(10) undefined.
https://www.seeker.com/should-we-give-robots-rights-what-are-the-ethics-of-ai-1792606542.html.

www.ingramcontent.com/pod-product-compliance
Lightning Source LLC
Chambersburg PA
CBHW072331290526

45794CB00002B/827